The Journey

William McRae

authorHOUSE®

AuthorHouse™
1663 Liberty Drive
Bloomington, IN 47403
www.authorhouse.com
Phone: 1 (800) 839-8640

Published by AuthorHouse 03/15/2016

ISBN: 978-1-5049-8392-1 (sc)
ISBN: 978-1-5049-8391-4 (e)

Library of Congress Control Number: 2016903718

Print information available on the last page.

Contents

Dedication

I dedicate this book to all people that have a dream to be successful, and to become world changers.

Acknowledgements

I'd like to give thanks to My Lord and Savior Jesus Christ for giving me the vision for this book.

- Timothy Thorpe: Whom God has used amazingly to edit this book.

- Vincent Graves (Digiworks Graphic Designs): To whom God has used in designing the artwork for this book which brings to life the message of this book.

Chapter 1

The Journey of Running

1. Inspiration

My inspiration to run comes from many sources. One thing I can say is that running three to four times a week gives me a way to meditate with God and recondition my mind, body, and soul. Secondly, I desire to maintain my health because I plan on being here to watch my family grow. Thirdly, my passion is running and sharing that passion is my way of giving back which is very important to me.

2. Mental Preparation

What keeps me running and not giving up is perseverance? It helps me deal with negative feelings or thoughts that promote fear. The truth is your mind and body have to work together to get a positive result such as winning a marathon or world championship.

Never have a doubt in your mind about your preparation because it can cause you to not believe in your highest potential when you are trying to reach a goal. Don't quit! Keep going and finish strong.

3. Goal Setting

In our society, goal setting has become a part of life at home, school, work, and social environments. Setting goals for yourself, is a way to motivate yourself to reach your highest potential. Whether your goal is losing weight, meditating, eating better, or improving your time, keep pressing to reach your personal goal. Run.

The main key to success is vision. Vision is a function of heart that we all must follow.

4. Knowing Your Potential

Each person that runs or fast walks performs at a certain level. However, everyone can't become a marathon winner. Even if you try hard each person has different strengths and weaknesses when it comes to your own personal abilities. Age and your physical health have a lot to do with your abilities when you run. Respect the body, but don't give up.

5. Time is an Essence

As the times change our bodies change with it. I remember when I was 25 years old. I was full of energy and I could run for days, Time passed, and now at 35 years young (older) I feel it more the next day.

I never quit, but I listen to my body more now than I did when I was younger. It's never too late to reach your goal but always make the goal realistic! Don't give up!

6. Physical Preparation

Endurance is determined by your muscle mass and how much body fat you have. Over the years I learned that how much muscle we have determines the oxygen level that you can use when you run. Your body weight determines your endurance or how long of a distance you can run. Physical strength also alters your muscles to increase your speed. The downside is that too much stress to soon can cause some serious injuries if you are not careful.

One thing I've learned during this journey is rest. Rest helps your body in a lot of ways.

William McRae

Running impacts your mind, body, and spirit. If you connect with all three, you'll be very successful. You will be able to improve your health, your thoughts, and most of all your spiritual connection with God.

"Success is a journey, not a destination. The doing
is often more important than the outcome."
-Arthur Ashe

Chapter 2

Runner's Questions for Me and All

1. What kind of runner are you?

2. Do you pray before you run? If so explain.

3. How do you prepare yourself before you run or race? Explain.

4. What is your biggest fear about running? Explain.

5. What does running mean to you?

6. Does your weight play a factor in your distance when you run? If so, explain.

7. Do you care more about winning the race or reaching your personal goal or your time in finishing the race? Explain.

8. When you run do you feel better afterwards? If so explain.

9. Is running a form of therapy for you? If so explain.

10. In a short paragraph tell me why running is most important to you, and why you continue to make it a lifestyle?

William McRae's Answers to the Runner's Questions

1. I am the type of runner that is passionate about running and meditating with God during my run. Running is a major part of my everyday life.

2. Yes, I pray before and after I run, because it's a lifestyle for me and it fuels my destiny.

3. My preparation is simple for any race because I am a runner every day. One thing I can say that I do differently is increase my miles and speed during my training and monitor my diet daily and eat a lot of bananas. That really helps.

4. My biggest fear of running is not being able to run anymore. It would be like a part of me died. It's that serious for me.

5. Running to me means everything for my health, mind and body.

6. I personally think your weight has a lot to do with your distance because the more you weigh the harder it is to improve your time and distance.

7. I care more about reaching my personal goal and my time in the race because I am a competitor and a finisher. Don't quit. Just do it. So I would say both are very important to me.

8. I feel like a breath of fresh air comes over me afterwards because running gives your body oxygen and helps digestion.

9. Yes, running is definitely a form of therapy for me and a big part of who I am.

10. Running helps me to release mental frustration, physical constipation and gives me freedom from the world. I hope my kids pick up running. It's very important to me that they do because it's a good way to achieve a healthy life and a spiritual connection with God.

Darryl Hairston's Answers to the Runner's Questions

My name is Darryl Hairston and I'm a friend of William McRae and I also work for him some weekends. I am a runner who just started a few months ago. Since I am fairly new to running I use the follow the leader technique to help get me started. That really helped me out the first couple of months until I was able to go on my own runs in town. How I prepare for my run I do a set of simple stretches to help decrease my chances of receiving an injury. I don't pray before my run but it seems like a sound idea.

My biggest fear about running would have to be getting struck by a vehicle. People drive all kinds of crazy in the United States, heck the whole world, so it's rather imperative to stay alert and keep an eye out during any run. Running has made an impact in my exercise routine. It's a great alternative to other routines out there and can help strengthen certain areas of the human body. Running can be rather relaxing to a lot of people.

One key thing about having a normal jog/run is a person's weight. My weight sits around 120 pounds due to my high metabolism. A heavier person would obviously have a harder time exercising. Another factor that contributes is if he or she is in shape. Being in shape really kept me running and when I kept running I kept increasing my good shape. Thanks to my weight I can do pretty good distances on my runs but since I'm still new to running I try not to overdo it.

One of the things I haven't done concerning my running career is participating in my first marathon/race. I want to be able to run a good distance without failing before I enter into one. If I entered a race, I would probably focus on surviving to the end and not much on winning or reaching a certain point.

After every run I can honestly say that I feel refreshed with a breath of fresh air feeling. At first it wasn't exactly like that. It took my body a few runs to become accustomed to it. I think running is one exercise that can become a good release to some people including myself. Running helps me think about other things and helps clear my head.

Running became important to me because it was another good way to stay in shape and also learn more about myself. For example, when I run sometimes I push myself to the limit and if something goes wrong my body will let me know. I would definitely make running a lifestyle due to the simplicity of getting up and moving somewhere whether it's in a gym, somewhere in the woods or in the city. Running has really opened my eyes when it comes to exercising because it can be fun.

Daryl Hairston

Daryl Johnson's Answers to the Runner's Questions

1. I would classify myself as a sprinter/ mid distance type of runner. That means that running the 400 relay (one lap around track) was my best contest in the realm of running, while anything that may exceed that could prove to be very challenging to me. This notion stems from reliving my yesteryears as it pertains to high school athletics, track and field, in which I joyfully engaged.

   I am a competitive runner who is willing to take a challenge however it may come. So when Mr. McCrae invited me to run with him in the 13.1 race in October of 2015, I accepted, but I did not fully understand what I was getting myself into. Initially I assumed that it would be something compared to a mile (if not less). He advised me that we would be doing an 8k run.

   At the time I didn't know how many miles that was. I quickly realized that my definition of what kind of runner I thought I was would have to be redefined after entering something of this magnitude. Ultimately, this running journey would answer that question for me one way or the other.

2. I do pray before I run. My mother always told me that God will never give you what you want if you don't open up your mouth and ask for it in spite of him knowing exactly what you're going to say even before opening your mouth. When praying I ask God to give me strength to endure the run, to embrace the run, to complete the run and in most cases to win the run. The most important thing I ask for when praying is that I make progress in the run in comparison to my previous attempts. As in real life, I believe that prayer helps me in the run. I take specific texts from

the Bible and write them down on pieces of paper and place them in the soles of my shoes for strength and comfort.

3. The first thing that comes to mind when talking about preparation for a run/race is dieting. After I determine the race date it becomes a countdown of detoxing my body of unwanted food and liquids that in the past gave me pleasure, but would ultimately have an unwanted impact on me and my overall performance in the race. I cut out all greasy processed foods and switch to cold cut sandwiches. My water intake increases while the "sweet teas" of the world decrease.

    Another part of my preparation for the run is endurance training. This requires a steady dose of me running in increasing increments leading to my ultimate mileage goal. My doing so, I am able to build familiarity with the physical demand. The distance becomes routine instead of stressful.

4. My biggest fear about running is regression. Regression is equivalent to failure in regards to not being able to build upon what I process and learn in the previous experiences (training, dieting, and prior races). These experiences collectively help prepare me to run while helping me endure any hardship that may prove challenging during my run. The fear of running and doing it in vain because of failure and the inability to reinforce those regiments established for the race are demoralizing and often times can become a major blow to my confidence.

5. Running means completion. The action of running is applicable in many aspects of my life. The obvious impact comes in the form of my heath. Running ensures that I maintain my physical fitness as

I age and makes me more disciplined to oppose things that are not fruitful for my body. Running makes me feel good about myself. It fixes my mood before I enter into my work environment. It helps me have the right attitude prior to interacting with my significant other; it sets the tone that I am ready to deal with the rest of the world and the stressors it may bring.

6. I don't believe that my weight plays a part in the distance I run. It's a matter of conditioning and a test of wills to endure the distance. My weight becomes secondary in my mind when running because the internal conflict that I have is a stopping vs enduring complex to arrive at the designated distance.

7. The competitive nature in me would place a priority on winning the race initially. However, in the grand scheme of things ensuring my longevity while being able to manage life's highs and lows comes first. The goal accomplished by running really attracts me more than any race win I could ever have under my belt. Enduring the run is an achievement in itself which is so fulfilling that it derives a sense of intrinsic motivation for me.

8. Every time I run it makes me feel better internally and externally. The internal perspective derives from a sense of accomplishment and self-worth. I feel as if I have moved a mountain when I have competed training for a race and the race itself. As for the external experience, my body feels great afterwards whereas I'm able to meet the physical demands of a 24-hour day. I feel better because my body feels as if it is in "ready mode" after I finish a run. My body feels lighter, overall I feel more confident in how I look, and my perspective on life generates a positive outlook on the things that I can and cannot control.

9. Running has not become a form of therapy for me at this time in my life, primarily because I use it to attain a desired physical goal more than anything else, Perhaps, as I get older and am able to identify with life a little more I would incorporate the therapy aspect more in my lifestyle. Through this I would be able to compartmentalize running in other areas of my life in order to be successful.

10. Running is important for me because it ultimately helps me focus afterwards. It helps me prioritize things I need to do daily in my life which in turn proves to have the most productive results. However, I have yet to make running a lifestyle because of my inconsistency. Obviously this comes with a slew of excuses such as procrastination, prioritizing, work schedule and the list goes on. Until I definitively decide to make this a routine part of my life, running is only going to provide me a temporary outlet of importance rather than on a permanent basis.

Daryl Johnston

Greg Echols' Answers to the Runner's Questions

1. The type of runner I would be classified as would be known as a mapper. I tend to keep track of new routes to try and log my distance. I am always using my GPS and distance logger when I run. I tend to stay away from doing the same route multiple times only to push myself to be able to complete a more challenging route.

2. I do pray before I run due to the fact one never knows what can happen. Also there are many obstacles and distractions that try to cloud your mind during the journey. I also have to pray during my run to keep me going. A lot of times during my last mile I may feel weak and fatigued but prayers always gets me through.

3. Preparation is key to being a skilled runner. I always prepare myself in advance for an upcoming race by working out. I normally workout 5 days a week with two leg day sessions intermixed with a 3 mile cardio run. Depending on the day of the event, I try to do legs so I have a 2-day rest period from working my legs prior to the race. This gives my leg muscles time to recoup, but they will not be as sore and quick to fatigue due to being worked. Also, this would not make them sore the day of the race. The cardio would be used to help keep my heart rate up as well as for me to pace myself at a good speed to finish without fatigue.

4. My biggest fear about running has always been hurting myself during a race. I fear I am going to mess up a leg or ankle and never be able to run again. Running is a passion I have and if I hurt myself to where I would never be able to do it anymore I don't know what I would do.

5.   Running to me means I am capable to conquer anything in life. Running requires loyalty, dedication, perseverance and consistency. Running for long distance is not something you can just wake up and do without practice. When I run I feel I can conquer anything in life once I reach the finish line.

6.   I feel weight does have some impact on the distance one can run but it's not truly the only factor. I know a few runners who are the same height as me but weigh a lot more than me and not muscle and they can run further distance than me. I feel it's more in the training more than anything. Someone who has trained their body more in cardio is going to have the greater benefit during a race. Weight does play a factor in the equation but is not the sole factor.

7.   I don't care about winning the race. I care more about reaching the goal. Winning the race is a privilege you earned due to the strenuous training you have accomplished, but reaching the goal is something you can never lose. I always set my mind on the goal of finishing the race whether or not I win.

8.   I always feel better after running. Running for me is a stress reliever. I can escape the world and relax my mind. I always feel great after a run because I am able to meditate and focus my mind on other things away from everyday life.

9.   Running is a form a therapy for me because it helps me relieve stress. My everyday life involves me working numerous hours and I hardly have time for myself. When I am able to run it helps me to relieve my everyday stress from work and to continue my day.

10. Running is important to me because it helps keep my mind focused and helps with daily stress. It helps improve my strength and endurance in my fitness goals as well. I try to make it a lifestyle throughout my life since it acts as meditation for me.

Greg Echols

"A journey is best measured in friends rather than miles"
-Tim Cahill

Chapter 3

Vison to Sight

Great Achievements Begin with a Thought.

"Nothing they set out to do will be impossible for them." Genesis 11:6 (NLT)

Man begins with a concept in his mind, something he believes he is able to accomplish; he joins his will and intellect to his imagination and then the power of expectation sees it though. Every thought is built in the spirit. Achievement therefore is a spiritual process.

Whatever can be already exists. God by His spirit spoke into existence all that is. He brought what already was in the spiritual into the temporal by the power of his word. "But there is a spirit in man: and the inspiration of the Almighty giveth them understanding." Job 32:8 (KJV)

Enlarging Your Testimony

What is the direct truth of the quality of your thoughts and the quality of your life? What do you think determines who you are, where you go, where you live, who you love and so on?

You will never have more on this journey of yours if you don't change your mind set. First you have to create the environment for your life. Your life is a reflection of your thoughts and meditations. When you meditate on success, you live a successful life. Never give up! Take the limits off, and most of all become a visionary.

"The real voyage of discovery consists not in seeking
new lands, but in seeing with new eyes."
-Unknown

Chapter 4
The Journey of Barber School

I graduated from Barber-Scotia College in 2001. I decided to attend barber school 5 years later. I began my journey of seeking different schools in NC, and I soon discovered Triad Barber School in Winston-Salem, NC. My first day of school I was a little nervous coming into a new environment, but after I showed Mrs. Kyles, the owner, what I can do my nerves went away.

Mrs. Kyles was like a mother figure to all the students at the school. She was the owner and an instructor at the school. She would always realize if you had any problems or concerns. She taught me a lot. She even gave me a side job waxing the floor of the school once a month. She had such a "Beautiful Spirit".

When I proved myself to Mrs. Kyles and showed her my leadership skills in class, she trusted me with the responsibility to teach class. In some ways, I felt that I was her favorite student, but she never said it out loud.

"Honesty helps the teller and the listener be willing to
feel bad before you feel good. Time = Worry & Fear"

My responsibilities at school were to teach the shave techniques class and to assist barbers with haircuts and styles. My overall experience at the school helped me to become the professional barber I am today.

I opened my own barber shop in Graham in 2005. When I arrived in Graham, my goal for my business was to put my customers first, serve people and my community, and make time for the youth by listening, helping, educating, and supporting.

Ten years later the business is still thriving and excelling in the community. Every day at McRae's Barbershop is a good God given day. Most of all, thanks to all the customers for their support of the business over ten plus years in business. Thank you.

"Only you know the path to your truth"
– Oprah Winfrey

"For those who love what they do, even working 18 hours a day, 7 days a week is not work at all. It is just fun."
-Unknown

Chapter 5

Barbering, History, Experience

William McRae

The Meaning of a Barber

A barber is a person whose job is mainly to cut and shave men and women's hair. A barber's place of work is known as a Barbershop. Barbershops are also places of social interaction and public discourse. Barbershops are also public forums. They are the locations for debates, voicing of public concerns, disseminating community information, and a place to be a blessing to others.

History

The barber's trade has a long history. Razors have been found among people of the Bronze age (ancient civilization) in Egypt. In the Egyptian culture, barbers were highly respected individuals. Priests and men of medicine are the earliest recorded examples of barbers.

Barbering was introduced in Rome by the Greek colonies in Sicily in 296 BC, and barbershops quickly become very popular as means to obtain daily news and gossip.

A few Roman *Tansores* (Barbers) became wealthy and influential running shops. Barbershops were the favorite public locations of high society. Most barbers were simple tradesmen who owned small storefronts or worked in the streets for low prices.

In the Middle Ages, Barbers often served as surgeons and dentists. In addition to haircutting and shaving, barbers also performed surgery and extracted teeth. These additional duties earned them the name barber surgeons.

19th century barbershops were influential in helping to develop African American culture and economy. Continuing through to the present, barbershops are an environment that can boost egos and be supportive as well as a place where phony men can be destroyed in verbal contests and other skill contests. It is a retreat for men to be themselves, and a way to escape from the world.

Barber Schools

Many states require a barber license in order to practice barbering professionally. The cost of barber school varies from state to state, and metro area schools in bigger cities tend to cost more than institutions in smaller areas. Brand names can also affect the cost of barber school. The costs of barber schools today range from $6,500 to $15,000 to complete. Barber license exam fees typically range from $15 to $50. Most programs are completed in twelve to fifteen months.

Barber Pole

The barber pole symbolizes blood and bandages. The red represents blood and the white represents the bandages used to stem the bleeding. Blue can either symbolize veins or a show of patriotism and a nod to the nation's flag.

The Experience of Barbering

I started cutting hair at the age of twelve in 1990 in my father's back yard. My first customer was my cousin. I gave him a high and tight fade which by the way turned out well for my first performed haircut. When the word got out that I could do a good job cutting hair for only $5, the community along with my family and friends kept me busy all the time. As a result, I learned good work ethic skills, and I appreciate learning this lesson at such an early age. It kept me out of trouble and focused on a positive future.

College Experience of Barbering

I arrived at Barber Scotia College (HBCU) in 1997. It didn't take long before everybody found out about the new barber on campus and the different types of styles and great prices I was offering. When word got out on campus, my dorm's lobby was full of people at all times of the day and some of the night. So many people were coming to get haircuts that it forced me to put a schedule up on my door so people. The dormitory supervisor talked to me and made an agreement saying if I cut his hair he would allow me to put a barbershop in the main lobby for free. (Favor) More people came through daily.

My college experience was fun experience but difficult. I was cutting hair in between classes, after classes, and the weekend and working full time in the evenings. I guess you can say I am a hard worker. Money was never a problem for me because I enjoy working hard to have the things I need and to be able to take care of my family.

My goal in college was to graduate in four years, and I accomplished it just like I planned (Faith). If you have passion about what you are doing, God will give you strength to persevere through any situation.

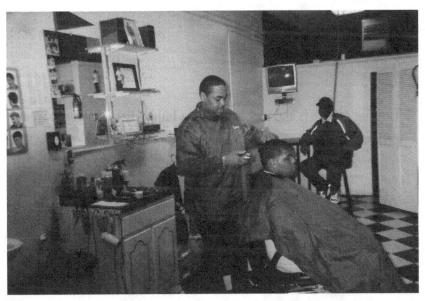

My First Customer, Jerry Paylor

"Loving others is the key to living a happy life. How you treat others is going to be an impact on your career and success."

-Jeremy Limm

Chapter 6
The Journey of Giving Back

On this journey of mine, I realize that giving is more important than receiving. I learned this method of life early on from a friend named Al. He is a type of person that is very active in the community, and volunteers his time and service for free to make sure people are treated fairly and make sure the next generation has a greater opportunity in their future. I learned a lot from him by watching and participating in community events. So I thank him for being the man he is and the risk taker that he is.

After gaining knowledge and learning how important it is to give back, I applied this method with my buddies years ago. I started a men fellowship group which was based on men discussing issues from marriage, religion, community issues, family and etc. The outcome of the group was to empower men in areas in which they needed help. They believed that there is strength in numbers to make a positive change in the issues that we face. I was inspired by the honesty of men, and the testimonies they shared. Looking back at that moment in life, seeing men come together for something positive was breath taking for me.

In today's society men are so hard to fellowship with because of family, job, and excuses have separated the male bond in society today, but if its drinking, drugs, and chasing women men come out for those things. So as time passed on I had to cancel the men's program, and I started a young men's mentoring program.

With that said years later I called a meeting with some close positive male figures that I've been knowing for some time. We discuss it how can we save the youth, since we can't save the older men. The guys and myself came up with a name called Reach 1 Teach 1 Young Men Mentoring Program.

The mentoring program is for sixth to twelfth graders. The program is designed to help young men become men and teach them skills they need in life. Some of the topics discussed include gang violence, family structure, appearance, health and hygiene, behavior, and most of all education. Every kid that takes part in the program is guaranteed to learn something from the 8-week class.

Reach 1 Teach 1 Mentoring Program Graduation

"Giving back involves a certain amount of giving up.'
-Colin Powell

Chapter 7

Journey of Mentoring

Mentoring has gained attention as a powerful tool to enable children of the program to be successful. The kids that are committed to the program are known to benefit from their involvement in these relationships. Research shows that people with mentors succeed with higher jobs satisfaction, stronger commitment to their families, and are less likely to fail.

I think it makes sense to invest in mentoring programs, so kids that need help can be better. In Reach 1 Teach 1 we are committed to diversity of young men, and teaching them key points in life.

What is mentoring? The original concept of a mentor was based on a character from Greek mythology, namely, Homer's story of *The Odyssey*. In this story, a goddess appears in different forms to help guide, protect, and support the journey of the main character within the story. This powerful figure that Homer classifies as a "mentor" has shaped our modern day expectations and perceptions of what a mentor does or more importantly what a mentor should do. However, it is helpful to have a realistic understanding of what is meant when the term "mentoring" is used in today's organizations. Mentoring is not about finding the perfect aid. A better way to describe it is a culture for service and serving for humanity.

"Tell me and I forget, teach me and I may
remember, involve me and I learn."
-Benjamin Franklin

Chapter 8
Mentoring relationships

Mentoring is about relationships that are mutual bonds of learning life skills between the mentor and the mentee over time. The relationship begins when both sides can be truthful, honest, and up front with one another. Also mentoring must be cultivated with participation on both sides. The next part is the attention to the need for developing more than one relationship. Mentoring that helps to support the needs of people, are not just for mentors, but instead requires a network of mentoring relationships. This is because mentoring must be diversified for the benefit of all mankind. So get involved because the rewards are priceless.

The kids that enter the Reach 1 Teach 1 create a bond between themselves and their mentors in the program. We all exchange numbers at the end of the program, so we can stay in contact with each other creating a bond or a brotherhood. Mentor's relationships can also provide acceptance and confirmation. Another way you can look at it is making connections with people who provide you with validation and support. Mentors give you knowledge, skills, experience, and overall support to the organization.

This acceptance can be critical, so remember, don't ever underestimate the importance of validation. Everybody needs a network of people who support their goals and ambitions.

Brandon Blackwell

Brandon Poteat

Ezekiel Williamson

Malik Tuck

Micah Johnson

Noah Clay

Ty'Rek Davis

"The mind is not a vessel to be filled, but a fire to be kindled."
- Plutarch

Chapter 9

5 Keys to a Successful
Mentoring Relationship

1. Vision

a. The act of power of sensing with two eyes, sight.

b. The act of power anticipating that which will come in prophetic vision.

2. Goal

The object of a person's ambitions or effort, an aim or deserved result.

3. Action

a. The fact or process of doing something typically to achieve an aim.

b. Cultivate: Prepare and use land for crops or gardening, try to acquire or develop quality, sentiment, or skill.

4. Trust

Firm belief in the reliability, truth or strength of someone or something believe in reliability, truth, ability or strength

5. Faith

a. Complete trust or confidence in someone or something.

b. Strong belief in God, in the doctrines of religion based or spiritual apprehensions rather than proof.

"Believing in yourself is the first secret of success.'
-Ifeoluwa Olayinka

Chapter 10

Journey of Biblical Principles

1. What you invest your time in is what your soul is connected to. (positive and negative)

2. How are unhealthy soul toxins and soul ties created in the first place? How you could end up cluttering your soul simply by the thoughts that you think? It is the energy that takes place when you give something your attention, or play things in your mind. Meditating upon it and speaking about it can be ways you connect to things in life.

3. The seed of thought is like the seed of a life. When planted, it will always result in an exchange of energy and therefore some kind of an attachment. Whether aborted or stillborn, an exchange of energy has taken place. The exchange takes place through investments time, energy, and actions in the form of thoughts, deeds or words exchanges. These can be both the intentional and unintentional.

Sometimes we can be completely oblivious to what we have attached to our souls something may have taken hold in our mind because we inadvertently paid attention to it for too long. I believe this why is it stated, "He that walketh righteously, and speaketh uprightly; he that despiseth the gain of oppressions, that shaketh his hands from holding of bribes, that stoppeth his ears from hearing of blood, and shutteth his eyes from seeing evil; He shall dwell on high: his place of defence shall be the munitions of rocks: bread shall be given him; his waters shall be sure. Isaiah 33:15-16 (KJV)

4. "Keep thy heart with all diligence; for out of it are the issues of life" Proverbs 4:23 (KJV).

"What goes in must come out." Our thoughts, intentions, motivations, secretly pondered in the heart as a desire or goal in our personal life will sooner or later reveal itself in the outer way of your life. Whatever we do in the dark will come to the light. God "will bring to light the hidden things of darkness" and not just our published motives." 1 Corinthians 4:5 (KJV)

5. Everything you see in the world began as a spiritual seed, a thought. The temporal realm has its roots in the spiritual. Grabbing a hold of this profound spiritual truth will enable you to make some creative connections that can transform your life. Once you understand your spiritual realm, you will instantly begin to activate the power of your thoughts, ideas, words, and prayers. It will enhance your future. "For as he thinks in his heart so is he." Proverbs 23:7 (KJV)

We must learn to harness our thoughts if we are to effectively reign as kings and queens in this earth. We must understand why we are here and where we came from as children of God. Every battle is won or lost in the area of your mind. If you do not take control of your inner thoughts, you will become a slave to the outer constrictions created in your mind! "For the weapons of our warfare are not carnal, but mighty through God to the pulling down of strong holds. Casting down imaginations and every high thing that exalteth itself against the knowledge of God and bringing into captivity every thought to the obedience of Christ." 2 Corinthians 10:4-5 (KJV)

Chapter 11

Journey of Family

Family is important to me because when your friends leave you, the only thing you have is your family in the end. I learned more over the years about what family really means. I have to include my business or direct connection with the people. I have a lot of genuine support and love from all my customers, so I consider them as family.

On my father's side of my family the love and support are stronger and they are supportive of each other, but I must say that the reality is we all have a lot of work to be done. Some of the few changes I would like in my family is love, respect, communication, spending time with each other, and most of all support for one another. If my family adjusts to changes, then I think my family will be complete and solid. My hope for my family is love, peace, and happiness.

Barbershop Family

"You don't choose your family. They are
God's gift to you, as you are to them"
-Desmond Tutu

Chapter 12

Key points to a Successful Family

1. Communication

a. The act or process of using words, sounds, signs, or behaviors to express or exchange information or to express your ideas, thoughts, feelings.

b. A message that is given to someone by letter, or a simple telephone call.

2. Support

To give assistance to or agree with or approve of something or someone and to give help or assistance to something or someone.

3. Prayer

a. A devout petition to God or an object of worship.

b. A spiritual connection with God or worship, as a supplication; thanksgiving.

c. The act or practice of praying to God or an object of worship.

4. Trust

A firm belief in the reliability truth ability or strength of someone or something. One in which confidence is placed.

5. Love

A strong feeling of affection and concern towards another person, as from kinship or close friendship. A feeling of kindness or concern by God or God towards humans.

"We don't need to have a long journey just to find love because in our home we have love and that's the family."
-Andreas G Matias

Chapter 13
The Journey of Marriage

In the beginning, I was introduced to my wife by an old friend. He told me that she was looking for a barber for her son, so I told him to bring them to the shop. So about a week later they showed up and introduced themselves. I had to hold it together because she was so pretty and she has such a beautiful smile that it was hard to make it through the haircut, but after I finished cutting her son's hair they both agreed that I will be the family barber.

Years later, after she became single from her late husband we talked about life and how each of us wanted our future to be. For the first time dealing with a woman, she made me feel that I could be myself and open and honest about who I really am and my family background. I felt that life was getting to a good place by hanging out with her. So after a couple more dates we decided to become a couple and move forward. Soon after making that decision I called a meeting to break the news to the kids and the family to let everybody know what our plans were.

So we dated for about 1 ½ years. I knew she was the lady I wanted to marry, but before I proposed to her I wanted to make sure she was on the same page as I was about the future. After talking to her I knew she was going to be Mrs. McRae because we agreed to share the same ideas and our plans were the same for the future.

My First Love Before My Love

My first love started with my grandmother who raise me and helped my dad make sure I was well taking care of.

I must say my first love begins with my grandmother. She taught me how to be respectful, trustworthy, responsible, and how to show and give love with kindness. These skills I always kept in my heart and I demonstrated them in my relationship with a woman.

In my teenage years I was far from thinking about marriage until I met my high school sweetheart. She was the first girl I wanted to marry. Here I am 16 to 17 years old thinking like a grown man proposing to this lady with a ring and I wasn't even a 100% sure because I was preparing for college. We talked and decided that when we finished college we can make it happen.

Time passed and slowly the phone calls were getting short, the desire was fading away from each other, so we stopped talking for an awhile. Then a friend of mine called me with the news I didn't want to hear.

He told me, "Your girl got pregnant."

My heart dropped. It took me a while to make the call to her and get her side of the story. When I got myself together I called and we talked on the phone first. Then I drove home from Charlotte, NC to see for myself. After all, that she had done I was still in love with this girl and was willing to marry this woman. However, the love wasn't mutual or the same because of her situation, so we both decided to move on with our lives and always remain friends.

Journey of Dating

During my college life experience, I can say I found out a lot about myself. When I dated women in college I realized that I needed to be with one woman not two or three. By me dating different women and not fully committing 100% to the relationship, I realized that I was creating soul ties with these women and playing with their emotions.

My grandmother always told me you reap what you sow. I started thinking in my head about how I need to take my life more serious, so I repented and apologized to each woman that I dated during this period of my life and sure enough they forgave me and we all moved on. I must say playing with fire will get you burned. Hurt People Hurt People.

"A good wife or a good husband is God given. They
come to fill the void in us as we also fill theirs."
-Terry Mark

Chapter 14
Things I Didn't Know Before Marriage

I must say I had no clue on what marriage is like until I got married. First, never go into marriage thinking you know everything about yourself. It takes you and your spouse or a relationship to determine who you really are. You can't figure yourself out by yourself. It always takes the help of a spouse or friend to get a full understanding of who you are.

Secondly, I still learn more today by listening to my wife rather than trying to take care of everything myself. I'm the type of man that works hard and rests less, but by listening to my wife about me getting more rest, it helps me be more productive and less stressed from all the work I do.

Thirdly, make time for your family. Don't just work yourself to death, and be absent in the home. Plan out family trips and family time activities so you can get the fullness of marriage and family.

Finally, have a balance between kids and your wife. Have a date night once a week and connect spiritually with your spouse. Having a foundation is good. It helps the marriage stay together and builds good communication skills with one another.

"An extraordinary marriage is not one without conflict. It is one where honesty, respect, and forgiveness set the tone for resolution."
-Kemmy Nola

Chapter 15
Things I Didn't Know About My Spouse

1. Communication

She struggles expressing her feelings to me because of her past. She said to me she never was a talker and neither were her parents. So I continue to help her get better with her communication skills.

2. Being Organized

She struggled having everything in order, but she finally came to me for help later on. I've learned that you can't change a person, only the person and God can change themselves. So I prayed for my wife to get better in the areas she struggles in. And she prays for me in my areas of weakness. So that builds strength for us to love each other more.

3. Forgiveness

I never met a person like my wife who forgives people so fast when they make her upset or make a mistake. Also, she doesn't hold grudges long which is a great thing. That's a good benefit for our marriage because it hurts me to dislike a person for a long time. Also we both share forgiveness towards people.

4. Love

I never knew what love really means until we got married. Real love begins with your relationship with God. Marriage can't work without God being in front of everything that you do. It took me a long time to figure it out. I can't do it by myself, and my wife told me that if we want the fullness of love it begins with Jesus Christ, because he loves us more than we love ourselves.

"Agape Love"

Marriage is all what you make it to be. Don't throw the towel in when the storm comes, just dance in the rain.

"Husbands and wives, recognize that in marriage you have become
one flesh. If you live for your private pleasure at the expense
of your spouse, you are living against yourself and destroying
your joy. But if you devote yourself with all your heart to the
holy joy of your spouse, you will also be living for your joy and
making a marriage after the image of Christ and His church."
-John Piper

Chapter 16

Things I Didn't Know About Myself Before Marriage

When I got married I didn't to know how much you have to give up of yourself to sacrifice for the ones you love. It was tough at first because I was so used to having things a certain way. For example, leaving home whenever I want to and not having to answer to anyone. Secondly hanging out with friends or just doing guy stuff without being rushed or timed. Finally, I was used to having a quiet house which is not the norm at the McRae home. Between the kids and the dogs, life is exciting every day. (Bundle of Joy)

Patience

Losing patience taught me to take my time in important areas in my life, such as family, life decisions, marriage, business and my children. I'm glad I've become the true definition of picture because it helps me be a better person for myself and towards the people I love. Being married changed my life for the good.

Wisdom

I've gained wisdom by watching my wife's approach towards situations. She is the opposite of me. She is the type that takes her time and then completes the job or task. Being married helps us both out in the weak areas of our life.

For example, going from 0 to 100 on things in life and just getting right to it is my personality. Her personality of moving too slow puts her in procrastination mode on important issues. She has to move faster so she can get right on what she has to do. We balance each other out to make each other better people.

My advice to married people is if you get married stay married because every year it gets better with time. Both sides have to do their part and both have to have God living on the inside of them to defeat the enemy when he tries to divide your marriage. Most of all in order to win the battle you must fight in prayer to protect your family. It works!

Love

I thought coming into marriage that I knew something about love. Shortly after, I've learned really quickly that things I thought was going to happen didn't but things happened a different way and it still worked out. I learned that love is demonstrated in many ways and just not the way I think it should be. Some of the few ways are:

1. Communication

Which means one way to express how you feel or your feelings.

2. Touch

The physical is another way to express your deepest feelings.

3. Support

Being there for someone other than yourself in ways like: finances, helping hand, conversations, prayer, etc.

4. Actions

Giving of one's self and how you show who you really are in a good or bad way reflects your character.

Mr. and Mrs. William McRae

"The greatest marriages are built on teamwork. A
mutual respect, a healthy dose of admiration, and
a never-ending portion of love and grace."
-Unknown

Chapter 17

Courageous Success Biblical Scriptures

Joshua 1:7 KJV

Only be thou strong and very courageous….

Joshua 1:8 KJV

This book of the law shall not depart out of thy mouth; but thou shalt meditate therein day and night, that thou mayest observe to do according to all that is written therein: for then thou shalt make thy way prosperous, and then thou shalt have good success.

Psalm 112:3 KJV

Wealth and riches shall be in his house: and his righteousness endureth forever.

James 4:10 KJV

Humble yourselves in the sight of the lord, and he shall lift you up.
Proverbs 11:28 KJV

He that trusteth in his riches shall fall: but the righteous shall flourish as a branch.

Proverbs 28:20 KJV

A faithful man shall abound with blessings: but he that maketh haste to be rich shall not be innocent.

Deuteronomy 8:18 KJV

But thou shalt remember the Lord thy God: for it is he that giveth thee power to get wealth, that he may establish his covenant which he sware unto thy fathers, as it is this day.

Proverbs 22:9 KJV

He that hath a bountiful eye shall be blessed; for he giveth of his bread to the poor.

My favorite scripture:

Mathew 16:26 KJV

For what is a man profited, if he shall gain the whole world, and lose his own soul? Or what shall a man give in exchange for his soul?

Important:

Philippians 4:13 KJV

I can do all things through Christ who strengthens me.

"For me and my house we will serve the Lord." Amen.

Chapter 18

Author Interview

What ambitions do you have as a writer? What is your goal as a writer?

My goal as a writer is to inspire people that read the book. I not only want them to be inspired but to take the message with them in a positive way and learn something from my story. I definitely want to impact kids, and show them that they can do positive things. I want them to not cheat life and to be honest and open.

What other books have you written?

Faith That Kept Me and *The Miracle in You*

Where can you get these books?

You can get my books on my website mrwilliammcrae.com, or you can go to amazon or any other major bookstore.

What are you working on right now?

The title of my current book is The Journey, and in this book I tell about my testimony, my journey, the things I've learned over the years, things that I'm growing to know. Some of the topics I talk about are marriage, how I knew things going in, and what I learned. Once you get into a marriage things change, and you have to adjust to the situation and make it work.

What drew you to want to write an autobiography?

I just want to tell my story because I come into contact with so many people, and just by listening to their testimony, I was inspired to want to tell my testimony. Standing behind a Barber chair, you're more of a listener than a speaker. I try to learn by listening more and talking less, but in this book I try to open up about my personal life just to be able to share some of my family experience and lessons learned growing from a child to my adulthood.

In the book, you have a chapter on being a barber. The barber plays a certain role in the community. He doesn't just make you look good, but the barbershop is a place where people meet. Do you see anything in being a barber that prepared you for being an author or wanting to tell your story?

Definitely. If my customers are pleased with their haircut, then I've done my job. In addition, if I can give an encouraging word then I've done my job. If I can give positive information or advice, then I feel like I've done my job. Being a barber is like being a resource center. People come to you for information all the time.

I'm sure you see a lot of issues that impacts the community. Would you say being a barber had anything to do with you wanting to give back to the community?

Yes. Giving back has been my mindset since I started working at summer camps when I was little. That experience taught me a little about giving back and working with kids and having patience. You are going to have to have patience being a barber. You are going to have little kids running around. You have to learn how to deal with certain situations when they come up. I thank God for the experience gained from going to summer camps and working at the camps through college. I just love kids and working with people. I'm just a down to earth type of guy.

When did you decide to become a writer?

I feel like I didn't decide it. I feel like God just drew me to it. I began writing about 5 or 6 years ago. I think that's how long it's been since my first book. I didn't want to write a book. I didn't want to tell my story, but when God tells you to do stuff you have to obey. You have to go ahead and go with it. You have to trust and believe that it's going to work. Some people are going to like what you say and some are not. That's life. I just have to do what I have to do.

Would you say that the Lord's leading is why you continue to write or do you have other reasons that you haven't touched on why you write?

I feel like in some ways writing is a ministry too. When you share your testimony somebody else gets healed through it, or they can relate to it. It might just be one word that they can take out of my message. It can change their whole life. If God gives me that type of power to impact others, that would be so awesome. It's not about self-gain because I don't need the money. I do the books because I love writing now. I didn't at first. The more I'm getting into it the better I'm getting at it.

I noticed the growth from your first book to the second book, and now looking at your third book I can see the growth. How do you think you've grown as an author?

I still feel like I have a lot more to learn. I don't know where this new book is going to take me but wherever it takes me that's where I'll end up. I'm just going to do whatever the Lord says, and try not to do things on my own. I always get him to guide me and show me the way.

What's the hardest thing about writing a book?

Having patience and finding quiet time are the most difficult aspects of writing because I'm busy being a father, husband, and business owner. It's just a lot. You have to deal with people and people counting on you for certain things. You have to be there for them too. I know it's tough but it's a sacrifice. You just have to do it, and I'm willing to make that sacrifice, in order to finish the task.

You think it's important to continue to grow and learn about marriage even though you've been married for a while?

I'm still a student of marriage because it's an everyday job. You learn something new every day. You just have to learn as you go. You have to know which buttons to push and which buttons not to push. I try to keep peace and harmony everyday as much as I can. You're unlikely to have a perfect life. It isn't going to happen, but at least give it a good effort every day. You thank God for waking you up and pray, "Help me god. Guide my steps. Guide my words, and protect my mind." You are going to need it because you know the devil is always busy. That's what helps me out.

Can you describe the cover?

A graphic designer, Vincent Graves and I, went through a couple of pictures and he came up with one. It's a man standing at the end of a boardwalk. He's at a place in his life where he's trying to make good decisions. He's trying to figure out which way to go, and as he looks out into the ocean he sees so many different opportunities. He can't even see the end of it standing at the end of the boardwalk. The guy is on a journey, and he's on the straight path, He has to stay focused. Don't look back. Keep going.

What advice would you give to your younger self if you could?

Continue to stay focused because I didn't learn that until I got in college. My parents said it, but you don't listen to them you try to rebel. My psychology professor pulled me to the side. He said, "McRae I see something in you. Always remember this one thing. Stay focused. If you are able to do that you will be able to go far."

That one word inspired me and it was like, "Go! Take off!" I just ran with it and kept it in my heart and mind, and wherever I go I try to take time to think and listen and pause for a minute. Don't make a quick decision. If you feel like something bad is about to happen, just stop for a minute and think about it. How is this going to affect me and my family? Stay focused. Go once you've made that decision. You are going to have to live with that decision, whatever it is, that's just my motto. It's what I live by. Don't move until you know it's the right move.

What advice would you give to an aspiring writer?

Tell the truth. Tell your story. Don't let anyone change you. Be yourself and it will work out. Make sure you're make an impact on people with your story whether its fiction or non-fiction. Make sure people can take something from it and use it in a good way.

How did the mentoring program start?

I saw a need for the community predominately amongst African American kids. The program is for all races of children, but we need it the most. I feel like those types of particular kids can relate to me because I'm African American and because of everything I learned over the years. They can pass it on to generations to come. Recycle knowledge, so they can do the same. It makes the world go around.

I just have a soft heart for children. I love them and I want to see them be happy and continue to get smarter and grow. I want to see them be something productive because one day we're going to get old and we are going to look back and these kids could be our next President or Secretary of State. Who knows where God is going to take them. We are going to have to look up to them. They are coming up behind us and they have to learn, and we have to teach. That's the way God designed it.

What are some of the things you have done in the mentoring program with the kids?

We took them on college tours. Community service is really big on my list. We need to do more of it. I feel like doing it one time a session out of 8 weeks is not enough. I feel like they should be continuously serving. We cover education. We teach them how to behave on a professional level such as communication, eye contact, dressing professionally or properly, not wearing saggy pants, not being a thug.

What are some issues you would like to see our leaders try to tackle?

Poverty is an issue here. Homelessness is another. Getting those people back on their feet, and rehabilitated with society is important. Get them some jobs and training. They need that. Sometimes people just lose it and go off on the deep end. They need resources. They feel like they can't talk to anybody because people are always brushing them off. You have to have the right people in position to make it work and be available to help the type of people who are dealing severely with that. I would say the crime rate needs to go down. Instead of using it for an economic reason, use it to really help inmates and young kids get off the street. Make it better. Have more resources for young folk rather than take them away. If you take them away, what are they going to do. You have all this time on your hand. Young kids are going to act up because they don't have anything else to do. They don't want to sit in school. They want to skip school and hangout. We have to be able to have a balance. We have to have people in position for those types of kids too. I call it "the over and beyond the call of duty" type of people. These are people that are willing to take that extra step to make it work. That's what the kids need. They need love. They need somebody to talk to.

What do you see as the state of the church today?

The Church needs to get in tune with the modern times and use different ways to attract young people because today young people don't want to sit in the temple but they would rather text you or email you. That's a good way to reach out to them. Churches today are doing a good job using social media and streaming. It's a need for that. You have to reach them right where they are. You have to go out there and reach them. You can't just be in the four corners and think it's going to work. The mission is out here. This is where it's at. You have to get out here with the people and do it. It's good to preach on Sunday, but you still have to go out. We are the body. We are one. We are going to have to represent Christ the right way. Some churches are doing it for the wrong reason, for financial gain or just power struggles. You have a whole lot of things going on, but I try not to get caught up on the negative. I try to focus on the positive. I just try to act in a way that makes a difference instead of being a complainer or gossiper or disparaging the ministry when we need to be building the ministry. Just do it the right way.

Printed in the United States
By Bookmasters